MY REASONS
AND
EXPLANATION

Crash Course in Contemporary Sociology: An Urban Perspective / Ideas and Disorders of Society

JONATHAN EDWARD OKELL MOORE ™

Doctor of Oriental Medicine

DEDICATION:

To Jasmine, Jade And Jaganath.

I Am Your Papi! And I Love you all!

This freedom is for you! Take it and grow on!

Foreword

One perspective and interpretation of what contemporary society acts on, that is what this first written word is made of. This production of work is based on notation frantically scratched on loose leaf paper like free-styled poetry during my Sociology course as taught by Professor Primoff at the University of Miami. The course assisted in giving words that equalled thoughts that in part articulate a foreign experience within a "society."

What follows is a compilation of notes mingled with thoughts regarding the perspectives of worlds created from thoughts formed within more recognizable than what I could grasp from without.

The observations of Life and arguments of wrong from right; that's what social studies are made for.

Table of Contents

Epestomology

Epestomology, or *Epistemology,* is the study of systems of knowledge. A system being nothing more than an organizational structure to create some form of order where none appears, a question arises as to whether the systems of knowledge are based merely on the dominance or submission of a person or group of people? Why is it not founded on higher ideals rather than consumption of economy?

A different introduction and review of many of the common terms, founding principles and examples of humanity expressed through sociologies is needed, however it must be assessed from a different perspective than often rendered.

Sociology is the study of social development in a demystified existence. A Modern man's experience is approximately 250,000 years old as "Homo sapiens," but what has 250,000 years of cognitive, physiological, and social development to do with individuals so massively confused by what seems to have been quantified into four centuries worth of cultural duress, coercion, conversion, inaccurate and deceptive practices? I guess that would really be subjective rather than objective as the definitive aspects to the underlying arguments are rooted in bias concepts viewed by those who remove the elephants chain from their minds with intent to deconstruct the oppression through analysis.

Emotion, often neglected in the study of civilizations social groups, is the defining characteristics that hallmarks the interests, inspirations, motivations, applications and manifestations of humanities social developments. Consider that emotion is the determining factor in all actions committed by woman, man or child. One person's happiness or joys motivate their actions centered around pleasure and that emotion derived as a result of the consequences or rewards gained determines will have further influence of how it is collectively viewed as "evil" or "good." Good, evil, right, wrong; all dualistic philosophical arguments existing in the realm of relevant relativity and applied moment to moment.

What remains decipherable or in need of less mystery when assessing one ideology rooted in oppression over another so greatly traumatized? Only a cultural amnesia and amalgamated ideology that affects the mental health and hygiene of the people influenced, indentured or in-slave mode.

What good would it serve for one to remember the injuries of another so far removed from when harm was first inflicted? What purpose would be served if the aim of such damage so long ago, presented no sight or sign of present affliction? Yet, the equation stands unanswered and undigested. The bitter gall of truth retarding in the ducts of sweet bliss and ignorance nevertheless lacks the potent conviction to inspire equal or greater retaliation... or retribution. The culturally foreign sociologists, psychologists and analyst of animal behavior often seem puzzled by the peculiarity of conditioning, partaking in the oddity so strangely entertained. I question why would a self proclaimed superior challenge an undeclared inferior if unless the opposite were true. A champion does not challenge, but entertains a challenge at leisure. Then it would be needless to identify the working producer who's buying capital was worth more of the service of the farmer or more of than that of the environmental field agent that would hold a service of greater value.

Religion as a Socially Engineered Science

A presumption exists that when humanity first became social, the first system of knowledge was based on religious beliefs. Volcanoes rumbling at an earlier time in humanity's development may have interpreted the activity as angered spirits. Perhaps there is a simplicity to it all that escapes the indoctrinated socialized mind, but maybe the answer quite simply is... the simpler, the better.

As a species advancing and learning the world from a western adaptation to eastern concepts via first person experience, the nature of humanity seems accustomed to accepting things still yet to be understood or observed, and as a whole, halts and reduces numerous possibilities into finite options that create a paradox in choice.

Secular knowledge is that which involves what the world now calls Science.

Science is the modern term for secular knowledge distinguished from spiritual knowledge as they coexist today in the forms of evolution v. creationism, or Abortion vs stem cell research. "Holcomb's razor" suggests that the simplest answer is the best answer.

Through the human experience, the progressive disenchantment of the world removes the once <u>magical</u> veil, and yet still poses no relative threat to the displacement of all religious knowledge.

From the Caucasian Eurocentric viewpoint of history, within the last 500 years, all knowledge was and is held by the church. However:

1. 14th C black plague strikes and exposes the Roman Catholic church which:
    A. Discredited the arbiter of all knowledge because it could not defend the faithful from illness and death.
    B. The Church was unable to keep its promise of healing those afflicted.
    C. The explanation of the Renaissance in the 15th century increased the "truth" by way of secularization
    D. Only in Astronomy did science stand alone with social concepts of God.
    E. FROM THE KNOWLEDGE AND PRACTISE OF ASTRONOMY, different sciences arise to explain nature.

Four disciplines:

Increase in secularization due to the "Black" plague

Industrialization transformed peasants to laborers, and the factory became the work-house or plantation, where monies were raised.

Emergence of Galileic ideologies (it's not nature / God, but man that causes it)

Caucasian European imperialism - Caucasian Europeans conquer many nations and form systems of control needed to reaffirm secularism

Among them:

- varying Shades of grey

- social methods of dealing with relative truth

- All questions are answered secularly via the Church

Concepts of Culture

The Culture of a society is a recipe for how that society functions. Culture is a way of life for any people; specifically, the human created strategies for adjusting to the environment and to those creatures (including humans) that are part of its immediate surroundings. These concepts affect and influence spiritual beliefs, moral and ethical codes, as well as the manner of dress and etiquette towards all manner of relationship whether of affection or disregard.

The core ideas, beliefs, values, language and material objects that arise from social life, are transmitted from one generation, through oral or written tradition to the next and are the basis for the identity of a cultural and acceptable social behaviors within it.

The two primary mechanisms humans use to survive are

- Instinctual or Innate skills involving the knowing of everything needed to survive (ex: birds, ants, spiders)

- Learned knowledge is what individuals are born without in order to survive, but can be learned or taught (ex: all mammals)

- Instinctual knowledge is set and has the inability to adapt

- Learned knowledge is flexible and can be applied to most of society any, if not everything

The Two types of social groups within society and they MUST be compatible

1. Material culture – uses technology and tools (ex: clothes, shoes, etc)

2. Non-material culture - ideas of nationality, religion, morals and values

Technology must be in balance with our beliefs and vice versa. *Cultural lag" theory suggests that the material culture almost always changes faster than our ideologies or beliefs. If the tools are overdeveloped, the values will eventually catch up as culture always continues to change.

Deviancy

Question: What happens when we don't behave? Deviancy is a social construct. No act is inherently good / bad as codes of morality are bound by specific culture.

1. Social Relativity is what is relative to a society, and how that society views actions as good or bad)

2. Defiance is based on normality created by the society, can be changed, but rarely are.

In most societies, most deviants are almost always <u>young males</u>, opposite old woman.

Types of regulations:

Social Regulations come from any rule prohibiting the killing of another human being, which protects us all. Elites, in most societies, create laws that protect their own power. Deviancy is the stepchild to contradictory social interest while Punishment keeps deviancy in, or under, control.

Kuzmet's Curve is an economist ideal that attempts to chart human inequality in human existence.

In Hunter/Gather Societies, very little is in equality. In agrarian societies it takes off. In the industrial age it reaches its peak, stops and began to show a decrease. Today, the curve has begun to rise again. When the most extreme part of the USA capitalist society began, laborers were needed to balance out the economic inequality, but in industrialized society, "man power" is needed less.

Dual Market Theory

Few high paying jobs requiring a lot of intelligence; many low paying jobs not requiring many skills.

There is an increase in downward mobility in today's society.

4 Major systems of human inequality:

1. The Master/ Slave system within the modern "new world" slavery, is very non-typical and unusual. There are many forms and shapes, however until the industrial revolution, slavery for the most part, took place within the "household"

2. Agricultural Revolution – Slavery became and was very profitable.

3. Empire-like societies based on human labor (slaves) continued until the Industrial Revolution, where a better form of labor arose. (machine / mechanized labor)

4. The most recent form of slavery on the rise is due to economic instability.

Inequality in the modern World

Civil War – North (Post Industrial) vs South (Pre-Industrial)

1. Economic and **not** moral war.

   - Slavery (coerced or voluntary) can be mild or extreme

     A. Permanent Slaves- Born/ captured

     B. Temporary slaves- indentured slaves, sold free for economic reasons.

     C. Inheritable or not? Child may or may not be slave because of "race" which is inherited, captured offspring may not become slaves. (transmitted or not)

D. Degree of control masters have over slaves.

2. Caste systems (Class system)

Indian caste systems – reincarnation allows for mobility in caste. No mobility; social caste is inescapable, and everything revolves around it. (Marriage, Labor, Religion, etc.)

Examples of Indian caste system

Priest – Reincarnation: Untouchable, Highest ranking members of society;

Warriors: if performed well in previous life as a peasant, then it could be expected to be born into a high caste in next life

Peasants: – workers that did the "dirty jobs"

Estate stream (feudal societies such as existed in England ("Robin Hood") and Japan (Samurai)

Nobility 3 half %, Clergy Church 7% Peasants 90%

Church also gives mobility to peasants with a "membership" such as altar boys, bishops, revered.

Class System (Open)

5 Characteristics

1. Combination of caste and meritocracy (power earned and deserved. ie. Personal achievements reflect status)

2. One class owns most of the means of production

3. Exchange labor for wages. (No one is paid their worth because it has to be rewarded less than its eco worth.

4. Sustainable Mobility- Can be born poor and die rich, and vice versa.

5. <u>A Middle Class:</u> that manages wealth for those that control that means on production. (factory manager)

Middle class is disappearing. (No middle class means greater gap between the wealthy and poor.)

Concepts of "race" within human society

Biologically speaking, there are no races within the human species. Humans do not meet the criteria for division of species because of permanent long-term genetic flow in humans which makes separation of species impossible.

"Race" is based on physical / biological (phenotypical/ Physically Identifiable) characteristics OR Ethnic-cultural characteristics. Race, is a sociological concept ONLY making it concepts mental of psychological, masked as biological concept. Though there are no biological traits, it does not mean there are no social traits. America is the only society that describes themselves in the form of percentages quantified as ¼ % white, 1/16 Chinese, ½ black in order to create a psychological profile of personality traits, financial worth and in the determination of association as the superficialities create stereotypes and archetypes of the company an individual might keep

No cultural traits are passed along with this information

- Race is important when people believe it to be "true" and important; however, a belief may not always be founded on knowledge of its contrived origins.

    1. Race is Not based on biological info.

    2. Race is a socially created code for groups of people to set themselves apart from others due to <u>socially defined</u> (actual / presumed) physical characteristics.

    3. We can construct categories in the absence of physical characteristics. (ex: religious association.)

People do not have to look different to be a race. Rules don't have to follow biological logic.

Q: What about race is important or constructed?

Racial codes may give some an <u>advantage</u> and impose disadvantages on others. A race "created" is seen as "inferior" to the observer and not "superior."

Only those in power create race as it is a code based on social inequality /disability subcategorized into economic class, gender and physical ability. The ideologies of race of presume one race being superior over an inferior creating a "we" versus "they, them" mentality.

It isn't the size that Matters...

The reasons for creating racial groups differ from those reasons that maintain them, however, these presumed differences are only advantages so long as there is a category of inequality; a "dominant" majority group and subdued minority group. Minorities lack power, and not the size. "Racists" exist only in the interactions with those "races" which are not isolated from another. Ethnic cleansing is a term for the murder of one race; i.e. genocide. The "marrying" or assimilation of races is when one "race" is enveloped into the majority, and the racial line vanishes, such as during the course of time of interactions between groups, a forced assimilation occurs where the majority encourages the minority to be like them. Economics and politics create interactions between the two groups. Ideals of racism are supported by the "belief" that the minority group is inferior in some form, and that the dominant group can "help."

Examples

1. Nazi Germany

- Jew-ish vs Arryian
    - both caucasian groups
    - The Jew-ish group in Germany were seen as a problem to Arryans who sought the preservation of their race, to which the death of the Jewish was a solution.

2. Rwanda, Africa

- Tutsi vs Hutu

- both Moorish / Berber groups

- Tutsi - physically taller, rich, urban, landowners

  o Hutus - wanted more land, education, and culturally opposite from both viewpoints

Native Americans vs Colonial Americans

- Indigenous vs European immigrants

- European immigrants wanted land and saw the natives as savages.

- European immigrants wanted them to work and also saw the natives as lazy alcoholics.

The foundations for race are flimsy, yet its superstructure is lethal. Sadly, in the west, ideologies of oppression rooted on the ignorance of a suggested are demonstrative of social and civil doom metastasized.

Gender

"Anatomy is destiny" - S .Freud.

- Genders are destined

- Sex vs Gender

  1. Sex - biological and anatomical functional code (male/ female)

  2. Gender - what societies create out of biological and anatomy categories (men / women)

  3. Basically, "Sex is what is between your legs; gender is what's between your ears. "

     One might ponder the possibility that biological females (bio-fem) may be instinctively attracted to biological males (bio-mal) for purposes of procreation. The possibility, meanwhile for bio-fem to be gender masculine (gen-mas) attracted to bio-mal gender feminine (gen-fem) may exist without distortion on the social norms (ex: 5'1" assured and assertive petite female with a 6'2 timid unassured hulk of a man) and that the appearance of physical gender based roles in reverse may and do exist in varying forms.

Some societies have more than (2) genders.

- Gender is a social construction, loosely modeled on sex.

- Some groups identified as "Indians" had "two spirit people" they were men / women as well as men and women and not androgynous in expression.

- Most societies are seen as patriarchal, and in these societies, the men decide what characteristics are fitting to gender. Men decide how men and women should act

- Few societies ran by women

- The most common cross cultural handicapped of female power is reproduction

- A unique fact of human reproduction- human offspring require more parental investment than any other mammalian species.

- This unique fact requires of men to protect women ensures the continuity of the species.

"Family" – Social institution of dependency, primarily women depending on men. Women not reproducing are seen as sterile. Women without a man are considered "lesbians" or that something is wrong with them, and therefore socially undesired.

Monogamy within Patriarchy allots all males access for sexual reproduction with 1 female. It is sexuality after all that is used everywhere to control Women. Sexuality harms women in many ways and benefits them in only one. In patriarchy, Male homosexuality is not tolerated because it threatens gender characteristics, whereas female homosexuality is tolerated more so, and would not be able to reproduce as it does in some contemporary modern society.

Through pleasure response, the manipulation of science for the purpose of conjoining a genetic biological bond to an altering social construct supersedes even natures social and specie-oriented program

Family

– The most important social structure.

Family provides food, clothing, shelter, and employment. Except-until recently, larger units of family were the result of one thing: marriage. Through the institution of marriage, individuals seek sexual ties outside of family.

Marriage – creates links with other families by becoming relatives. Essentially, men create societies by exchanging women and Never the male.

5 functions of the family in human societies:

1. Economics of production by the family provides jobs, a means for survival, and families large in size resemble a company / employee. The Industrial Revolution took work outside of the family structure, and placed it in factories / offices, and stripped family of economic functionality trading it for a contemporary economic unit of consumption. Families survive better in small sizes for consumption purposes. Family members working outside the home obtain more power as they now become the providers of survival necessities.

2. Monopoly and regulation of sexual behavior plus family is only place regulating the intimate relationship between men and women. The Family is only place inhibited by both men and women.

3. Where children are raised to maximize their survival and mortality, women are dependent on men, children are dependent on parents and the head of household is held responsible by society.

4. Children raised by biological relatives have best chance of survival principle of legitimacy most soc. Demand that every child have a

sociologic link / sponsor between the child the society. Social Sponsorship equals last name.

5. Once human beings become stationary, the stress of virginity becomes important for the identification of inheritance purpose to the legitimate heirs with other determining factors.

   A. Socialization of the young – where we learn language, religion and economics of the larger society.

   B. Replication of patriarchal control- intuitions in which men institutionalize control over women. Men continuously exercise influence over women generationally. Male children observe and learn control / dominance over women who learn through conditioning to be dominated / controlled. The basis of which is for practical / political reasons.

   C. Affection via companionship were not essentially important historically until recent years. Husbands were unaffectionate towards wives, however, within families' emotional needs met. A society's institution for emotions only function really works in Caucasian American / European societies. In these societal structures:

   - Family is economically viable;

   - Do not act as sexual regulators; and

   - Currently, parental socialization of children no longer occurs due to work, exchanging paid supervision of children instead of doing it ourselves.

   - Marriage is a ceremonial transfer of a woman given away by her "old master" (normally the father) to her "new master" or mister (the husband).

Constructing Social Institutions

Q: What are the natures of these institutions?

Institutions are made up by complex of status and each status has a role. Human beings function in a society based on status with specific role functions to perform (ex: bob is a good father; father = role; status / performance = good). Social Interactions occur when a person performs a role(s) based on status interactions with each other. "Status" is the basis for social life. (Example: someone's friend, lover, husband, father, etc) in which we do the most to fulfill the description to get along.

Two kinds of status

1. Forced status - Gender – male must act as a male, supposedly (the ideology of race)

2. Achieved status- Title - ex: doctor, student, sociologist etc.

    Some status is inescapable and come in pairs (reciprocal; McD's employee, and McD's customer; brother)

Master status

- gender - no choice on the character to be played (ideologies of "race")

*status and their roles make life possible because a) roles are performed smoothly; and b) knowledge of other status is communal (known by all).

Human beings interact with each other based on role of status therefore "stereotyping" is the social normality by identification. Role strain is the tension within the roles contradicting each other (father- dad, discipline). Role conflict occurs when trying to perform two roles simultaneously (ex: being on a date and parents are eating in the same restaurants) It can also occur in the absence of the father as well.

There is No place within society that doesn't require a status role. Scripts can change, but only to different ones, the play never stops. The show goes on.

Q: Why are we controlled by constrain?

In early societies, the environment most likely dictated an individual's ability to do what they wanted (ex: cold weather, mango season). With growth of agriculture, the notion of the "state" emerges. The "State" is an institution that intervenes and regulates daily lives with rules and regulations. (Controls marriage, dog license, even sex, ie: pre-maturity sex, driving at certain ages, etc). After the Industrial Revolution, the capitalist looks to control means of production much more. Strains in theory controlling social activities.

The Clock has regulated and measured time. (ie: workers show up at 8pm). The "Iron cage of rationality" suggests that humans are losing ability to choose their own lives by the rules of society which looks to make it more rational or efficient.

Bureaucracy is a system based on quantification and efficiency originally restricted to business but has branded out to run countries. Bureaucracy is made up of titles (pres, vice pres, sec, salesman's, manager) and with such granted authority / power of the role or subjection to a role. As long as it is still in that position.

6 principles of bureaucracy (power and authority)

1. High division of separation of labor. (no title has all the power)

2. A clear chain of command (military rank structure is perfect example)

3. Rules and regulation (what you can do and cannot do)

4. Impersonal relationship structure (it is not the person that is important, but position / title)

5. Clear career ladders (clear career paths to greater position: see board of directors, chairman, vice pres, pres* no skipping)

6. Efficient (a system revolving around numbers ie: ssn, drivers license etc.)

Social function is constrained; only choices available are those provided for us and one of the provided must be chosen.

Biological basis for human sexuality

The Assumptions about any sexual reproducing organism:

1. Basic drive is the notion of reproduction (genetic procreation)

2. Survival of the fittest is wrong! Reproduction ensures survival.

3. Survival and reproduction are not the same.

Above all, most of us, most of the time, want to reproduce. Mammals are sexually reproducing organisms. In this basic function of all mammalian species:

1. Cooperation between male and female relationship strategies for sexes are differing which create struggle... for comprehension and / or communication to engage in sex and achieve reproduction.

2. Gender competition – the human Male has unlimited capacity for reproduction as the biological function of the male species is to produce new genetic material for sexually available females.

3. Sexual availability is based on a woman's physical appearance to reproduce. If she is not already pregnant, she therefore appears available to engage in sex, though reproduction may not occur.

Human males in particular have the ability to reproduce new genetic material as often as possible. This allows them to maximize quantity of mates. A female has a limited capacity for reproduction not to reproduce as often as possible, but with the best genetic material that is also sexually available to her.

*Maximizing quality of mates

1. Good genes are expressed in physically traits.

2. Good parental investment.

Contradiction – In the animal world, monogamy is very rare. The exception to this is that the majority of humans like monogamous reproducing relationships. Monogamy suits certain cultural needs, but the advantages for females.

Not all males reproduce, but almost all females do reproduce. Essentially in evolution, most male genes never get passed on. Why?

50 / 50 (male / female) ratio though monogamy balances human sexual reproduction, however it prevents best suited males from only mating with females.

This helps to explain why male homosexuality genetically could not continue to reproduce as undesired males would not be permitted to reproduce without deceiving the society or female. Through cause and effect, the restrictions and social restraints that look down on homosexuality have created new and even more social deviants in the form of transgender. Again, these concepts would not be socially acceptable even in the male dominated society that is only an extreme in comparison to its female dominated society. Then again, what are male- / female- dominated societies but social groups ran by the most influential of the sexes? It can therefore be presumed that the perpetuation of homosexuality and the mass indoctrination of "acceptance" advertisement is a method to control population sizes of ethnic sub-cultural capacity.

Through Natural Selection, Power and gene compatibility equals attraction and most physically powerful. Human Social Selection is based on Economic and power compatibility. The more capital / dependability equals more powerful. Human Females are almost always distrusting of "good looking" men because they can be "untrustworthy," except in the cases of powerful females that look at the best genetic material. If human females behaved like females of other species, monogamy within humanity, more than likely would not exist.

The social pressure of monogamy and reproduction causes human females to be unlike females of any other mammalian species.

1. Human females appear to be continuously sexually accessible.

2. When females are fertile, certain tell-tale signs are visible however, human females have developed concealed fertilization, which maximizes human male stability (sticking around).

3. Women have developed traits that perpetuate monogamy and propagated in raising children quickly throughout the species.

Children

Only human birthing is a problem because of the human females gait (hips) being to narrow, and the heads of the children usually are too big.

*Human children, comparatively, are born premature in which the women are "stuck" raising the kids for longer periods of time which equals longer dependability on males.

3 conclusions:

- Essentially in every society, female sexuality is constructed to suit male needs. (Presently: women attract men with the proposition of trading genes for protection. 1 heterosexual 2 mothers).Normal women is with a man, without paying a price unless she is socially in the position of power financially.

- In societies where women become economically independent, they are more able to define their own sexuality. Women left alone would look different today.

- Based on the aforementioned reasons, if a woman wanted to be in the position of "power," they must give up (to some degree) motherhood.

A. Structure of Human Family

The Human Family structure is influentially affected by outside structures.

The economical structure of the human family is determined by where they live, and the economic stability of the members with the family. Most societies are monogamous while others are polygamous

1. Polygamy is not about sex: it is primarily about economics.

    - Polygamy is the practice of men having several wives. Men have more than 1 wife in a society where women's label is more important. Most occurrences in rural areas tend to be the most beneficial. Additionally, because 2nd and 3rd wife may act as an assistant with maintenance of household duties, this always benefits the man.

- Polyandry is the practice of women with several husbands (usually 1 wife/ 2 husbands), and the husbands are usually brothers. Male offspring is usually interchangeable (unidentifiable) between the brother. Why would brothers share a wife? To ensure the inheritance is passed to a genetic heir. Example: a very poor men that do not have enough land, poverty forces them to share a wife. Split Inheritance.

2. Size of Family.

- Usually determined by economic standing i.e. if the family is large, they usually have more land, property, wealth, (power) <u>easily attained in a rural area.</u> Economic fate is not a necessity in urban lifestyle, whereas in rural areas, it is, therefore the family size is based on the same.

- Arranged marriages are not unions of 2 people, but two families, therefore attraction is not a factor. Divorce is not an option. In romantic relationship, divorce is higher, and fails more than arranged marriages. Divorce is 50/50 in romantic relationships and 10 % - 20 % likely to occur in an arranged marriage.

- Women = labor sources, families are economic organizations, and when one family loses a daughter to marriage (union of family) a "bride's prize" is necessary to replace the loss of labor.

- The family receiving the added labor (daughter in law) provides a <u>Dowry</u> to maintain the added labor (essentially to fund the bride).

Rules of who you can and cannot marry:

Exogamy dictates the exclusion of certain people from marrying each other - namely family marrying family (incest), as it creates complication with family hierarchy; ie. Confusion of status of a son marrying his mother – he is her son and her husband.

Endogamy dictates and limits to who people marry within the group while excluding a few (Jew marry Jew, but not their mother, father, sister, brother, etc.)

Furthermore, members of a family are further prohibited from engaging in homosexuality as same-sex relationships reduce inheritance restricted to the conditions of biological reproduction and places a strain on social "gender" based roles.

B. Education

Higher education In the U.S

- College / Universities

- Historical problem

- Caucasian American Universities are based on Caucasian European counterparts. Europe's emphasis on educational system that caters to mostly the wealthy nobility.

American Universities catered to the sons of the American Elite (wealth/Politics).After the building of Universities that catered to the sons, a small wave catered to the daughters of the American Elite. In the 1950's, American Society opened doors of higher education to the sons and daughters of non-elite, but the "need" for the two differed greatly. The model of liberal arts education suits the needs of social elite very well, but today they act as a "buffet" of knowledge broadly conceived as education.

American Universities Intended to broaden intellectual horizon, however:

1. It was not designed or intended to prepare students for occupation.

2. American universities did not provide an extra 4 years to become educated in a liberal fashion.

3. Cost was no object, prior to a more educated public was needed, to which the same educational model was prescribed for social elite. Today, students attend college to reach a better economic standing. Leisure time has shortened, and education is taught in this manner.

Roman Circus – young adult goes to college, prolongs education and adds 1 years of "fun time." The young American adult rarely has cultural aspirations, only economic aspirations which are costly. Most students graduate in debt.

Most students today are not pursuers of knowledge; instead they seek financial security negating passion for the simplicity of life.

Population

The largest concern of most by sociologist is world population. Humans reproduce 200(k) a year, and for hundreds and possibly thousands of years, humanities population had never reached 1 Billion in population until 1850.

In the 1850's, for the first time in history humanity globally reached 1 Billion people. In 250 years, we added 5 - 7 Billion people and by the year 2050, approximately 8-9 billion people are expected to be alive. It is possible however, from the perspective of the food producers, 9 Billion will not be sustainable and ironically, it is possible without current race based ideology, but these ideologies do exist.

Within the American society, it is illegal to promote the use of contraceptives such as condoms, birth control, but social ideologies are what prevents the occurrences.

Q: Why did it happen? What caused the increase in population?

A: Demographic Transition theory.

Human population was held in check by very simple reason; Humans were born with high fertility rates, but also high mortality rates.

Today taxes equal lower fertility among the social elite. Humanity prior to the 1850's were affected by:

1. Infant mortality rate

2. Very strenuous lifestyle – hunting – high adult mortality rate.

3. Very short lifespan – most people die in their thirties

    **even the time in which women reproduced were very short

Today, more food and healthier people equals longer life, higher fertility rates, lower mortality rates. Fertility Rate have stayed the same. Urbanization began after the Industrial Revolution and a created cost defiance associated with children which controlled fertility.

- Spikes in Population do not occur throughout the world, but in countries where fertility control is unaffordable, does it happen the most.

- Rural poor countries have the higher populations.

1. Children are economic security and provide care for elderly. Men control reproduction, women only reproduce, they have not controlled it.

   - Immigrants keep urban populations (and their replacements) rate (minimum of 2 to 1) stable.

   - Bigger Social Security Issue = Older population (Up), Younger population (Down).

   - Best form(s) of contraceptive:

     1. No poor women

     2. Educated women

     3. Independent women

     4. **Population emphasis on poor countries.**

Population problem of rich countries are dependent on fertility rates being too low. How do you increase population?

Spur to increase fertility rate (*very hard)

   - European Social solution – Governments make it less expensive to have children with incentives. Ex: free daycare, free medical care, etc.

   - U.S. Social Solution – No incentives provided to keep fertility rates low and do so through immigration.

2. Reproduction by immigrants from poorer countries stimulate members of wealthier classes / citizens to reproduce more frequently.

Most Men / Women / Children live in poor countries throughout the world

Several structures for trying to control fertility rate

My Reasons And Explanations

1. Heterosexual intercourse – control reproduction through delayed marriage.

   - Postponement of sexual activity by at least 2 years

   - Negative affect- if sexes are not touching it is considered "safe sex" which reduce STI rates. Europe has given up controlling people from having sex

2. Intercourse permitted; as long as unwanted pregnancies are controlled (*if government cannot control sexual behavior, it can control the outcome through a) knowledge to use pregnancy technology; or b) have to afford pregnancy technology.

3. Abortion technology – measure used after preventative pregnancy measures fail, include the possibility to control live births. * The poor women aborting are usually rural migrants to urban areas.

4. Infanticide – Measures used in poor countries if abortion technology has failed, and killing the child is another socially accepted option.

5. Very rigorous "scripts" with one commonality: accidents usually occurring to little girls, then little boys.

One "Script": followed by women in poor (labor intensive, economically poor)

1. Does laundry with baby slung on her back

2. Goes to river and leaves the child on a rock in the middle of the river, and if nothing happens to the baby, the mother takes the baby back to village

3. Repeated again until the baby disappears on the rock

Problems for controlling fertility

(Almost always)

1. Men primarily are uncooperative in contraceptive usage

2. Most poor women are unaware of fertility control; or

3. Most men and women are too poor to afford the fertility control

4. Men will not let anything mess with their offspring, especially women in control of their fertility.

5. No access to clean water source to take contraceptive

Why are men into having children?

1. No cost to have children and economically useful

2. Children are social security when parents get old

3. Children can be a source of status

Theory of Great Disruption
(Proposed by Fukuyama)

A conservative view of social change in American society. The central premise being that when society becomes transformed by a new society, the old ones have to be deconstructed before a new one is instituted.

Break an egg to make an omelet.

1960-1990's – Theory – American society, as an industrial organization, began to fall apart around 1960's (Hippie revolution) moving toward a post-industrial society. By the '90's, America's post-Industrial society, began to fully take shape in preparation to abandon old ones that no longer applied, however, those new rules haven't been made yet.

5 key indicators of disruption

1. High crime rate – Kill, steal, rape in America are very high with new prisons being built, greater "wants" = greater defiance.

2. American families' institution decline, divorce rate increase, marriage rate decrease - when economic structure changes the family structure changes as well.

3. Lost trust in governing institutions – distrust for everyone , and everything; people have to prove trustworthiness in this present day where confidence in society has been lost

4. Social Sexual Interaction change – much less permanent, much more loose, yet more restricted to different arenas - reduced sexual interaction

5. Friendship ties have become weakened. – Friends yesterday are less committed / supported in today's seemingly available society

   - Fukuyamas conclusion- Societies will become much more independent, and not happier with their independence.

- Negative trends are weakening the social body and values intimately connected with creation of new ones.

Technological changes have brought on new types of relationships. The desires of today support independence, distrust of authority and the increased wants to be masters of our own destiny; however, we want community.

Community provides authority and rules that contradict independence with weak restricted loose communities in name / title only.

Fraternities, Sororities, team favorites act as "communities" that bind us together, and out of the usual "social space."

Mcdonalization

The concepts that make McDonald's (a franchise) efficient, are being adopted by society. Efficiency is costly, and productivity determines value.

Fabre was the first Sociologist to worry about effects of modern society on human beings and their social freedom. His Antecedent – Law of Iron Cage of Rationality - was based on the fear that sustain our existential choices / options by an ideology of rationality. Life wasn't standardized. The Industrial revolution (emergence of factories) was the preliminary causative affect of human beings losing control of their life ie: time schedule – clock in- clock out.

The clock became a social symbol that not only measured time, it gave a concept of "hive mentality" with workers marching to the beat of one drum. It is Bureaucracies first institution to arise and meet the ideology of uniformity. (1ˢᵗ social constraint). Assembly line education, cars, etc. Efficiency in this manner, leads to unquestioned value.

Mcdonaldization of human society is becoming similar because they are being increasingly structured and managed by the same principals as McDonalds or any other fast food restaurant.

Rationals taken to extreme always result in irrational consequences

4 Principles of Bureaucracies

1. Efficiency - Goddess of modern societies. (morally efficient) Efficiency does not mean it is a good thing.

2. Uniformity - Each model resembles the last one created to be used interchangeably creating a system of efficiency.

3. Automization - the use of machines which do all the work and humans service the machines. Technology sets boundaries of tasks that are possible and impossible.

4. Predictability - removes risks, or packages them in safer ways.

In closing, ultimately, human societies will adapt, evolve, conform and rebel as the society will permit is still based on the emotional maturity of its members. After all, the members matter most to the life of the society and so we must now observe, diagnose and treat the individual nature of Humanity as unique expressions independently codependent on the nurturing of its society.

LOVELY GODDESS PRESS, CORP

PUBLISHING

MIAMI FL

Goddesspressandprint@gmail.com

Copyright © 2017 by Jonathan Edward Okell Moore

ISBN-13:9781981949687